An Inevitable Journey

An Inevitable Journey

R.M. Wood

Matador
Unit E2 Airfield Business Park,
Harrison Road, Market Harborough,
Leicestershire. LE16 7UL
Tel: 0116 2792299
Email: books@troubador.co.uk
Web: www.troubador.co.uk/matador
Twitter: @matadorbooks

ISBN 978 1803135 816

British Library Cataloguing in Publication Data.
A catalogue record for this book is available from the British Library.

Printed and bound by CPI Group (UK) Ltd, Croydon, CR0 4YY
Typeset in Arial by Troubador Publishing Ltd, Leicester, UK

Matador is an imprint of Troubador Publishing Ltd

ACKNOWLEDGEMENTS

Thanks to the following for permissions:

All Creatures.org,   Binford and Mort Publishing,   Bloodaxe Books,   Laura Chester,
Oriana Conner,   The "i" newspaper,   David Higham Associates Ltd.,   Desmond Morris, F.L.S.,
Colin Parkes, O.B.E., M.D., F.R.C.Psych,   Scribner, a division of Simon & Schuster Inc.
"The Sunday Times" newspaper,   Ann Widdecombe, (former M.E.P.)

Every effort has been made to trace the copyright ownership, where applicable, of the extracts used in this book,
however a few have proved impossible to trace. (A log of the process is on file.)

Dedicated to
Sweep, Daniel, Buttons,
Cinders, Solo, Domino and Billy
for whom I travelled this journey

By choosing to be a pet owner, we choose, almost inevitably, a bereavement.

This "inevitable journey" through grief may take the form of a direct route or the way may be missed and parts of the journey repeated. The road may be bumpy and the time taken to travel may vary greatly. Sometimes a bereaved owner may even find themselves unexpectedly back at the beginning. The stages may not follow the line of this journey at all, but become jumbled.

Whichever way the journey is undertaken, I hope the following way-markers will offer some understanding, comfort and hope to all who travel.

"The misery of keeping a dog is his dying so soon.
But to be sure, if he lived for fifty years, and then died,
what would become of me?"

Sir Walter Scott – Scottish Poet, Playwright, Historian (1771-1832)

INEVITABLE BEREAVEMENT

"There is sorrow enough in the natural way
From men and women to fill our day;
And when we are certain of sorrow in store,
Why do we always arrange for more?
Brothers and Sisters, I bid you beware
Of giving your heart to a dog to tear.

When the fourteen years which Nature permits
Are closing in asthma, or tumour, or fits,
And the vet's unspoken prescription runs
To lethal chambers or loaded guns,
Then you will find – it's your own affair –
But … you've given your heart to a dog to tear.

When the body that lived at your single will,
With its whimper of welcome, is stilled (how still)
When the spirit that answered your every mood
Is gone – wherever it goes – for good,
You will discover how much you care,
And will give your heart to a dog to tear.

We've sorrow enough in the natural way,
When it comes to burying Christian clay
Our loves are not given, but only lent,
At compound interest of cent per cent.
Though it is not always the case, I believe,
That the longer we've kept 'em, the more do we grieve
For, when debts are payable, right or wrong,
A short time loan is as bad as a long
So why in Heaven (before we are there)
Should we give our hearts to a dog to tear "

"The Power of the Dog" from "Garm – a Hostage" 1899

Rudyard Kipling, English Poet, Novelist (1865-1936)

"A still small voice spake unto me,
Thou art so full of misery,
Were it not better not to be?"

"The Two Voices", 1833-1834
Alfred, Lord Tennyson, English Poet (1809-1892)

"Pain – no pain intrudes; but calmly,
With no heavy laboured breath,
Sinks the soul to rest; revealing
But a passive, easy death."

"Euthanasia" Lavinia J. Lawrence, American Poet
"Euthanasia and Other Poems" published by Turner & Co. 1870

"So, we come to the end of the road. In the midst of
what seemed still his puppy-hood – so young and
playful was he in spirits – the dear Beau was taken
very suddenly ill, and after a sad vigil of only nine
hours, he breathed his last and just fell naturally
and peacefully asleep. Our only consolation was,
he did not appear to suffer much pain and
for this we were truly thankful.
So, he passed from our sight, leaving only happy
memories which will cling to me to the end of my
days, and with grateful thanks in my heart
for his loyalty and devotion."

"The Love of a Dog", circa 1941 Joan Gratiana Darell, English writer (1900-1985)

"Then from the wood a voice cried: *Ah, in vain*
In vain I seek thee, O thou bitter sweet;
In what lone land are set thy longed-for feet?"

"Missing" A Book of Verse (circa 1870)
William Morris, British Textile Designer, Poet (1834-1896)

"Lying awake in the dark that night, unable to sleep, he thought that he would have given anything to feel the heavy thud on the bed that used to announce the old dog's arrival. How extremely unloving and intolerant he had felt so often, waking in the middle of the night to the relentless shoving and pushing …

Tonight, he reflected wryly, I'd give him the whole bed! I'd even sleep in the basket myself – if only he would come back".

"The Incredible Journey" first published 1961
Sheila Burnford, British Canadian Writer (1918-1984)
Permission granted by David Higham Associates, Ltd.

"Grief is the price we pay for love
And usually this price is worthwhile."

Colin Murray Parkes, O.B.E.,M.D., F.R.C.Psych, British Psychiatrist and Author (1928-)
permission granted by Dr. Parkes
extract from the introduction to the first edition of "Bereavement: Studies of Grief in Adult Life"

Sweep 1951-1963

"Pet was never mourned as you,
Purrer of the spotless hue,
Plumy tail, and wistful gaze
While you humoured our queer ways,
Or outshrilled your morning call
Up the stairs and through the hall –
Foot suspended in its fall –
While, expectant, you would stand
Arched, to meet the stroking hand;
Till your way you chose to wend
Yonder, to your tragic end.

Never another pet for me!
Let your place all vacant be;
Better blankness day by day
Than companion torn away.

Better bid his memory fade,
Better blot each mark he made,
Selfishly escape distress
By contrived forgetfulness,
Than preserve his prints to make
Every morn and eve an ache.

Housemate, I can think you still
Bounding to the window-sill,
Over which I vaguely see
Your small mound beneath the tree,
Showing in the autumn shade
That you moulder where you played."

"Last Words to a Dumb Friend" (1904) Thomas Hardy, English Novelist and Poet (1840-1928)

"After great pain, a formal feeling comes –
The Nerves sit ceremonious, like Tombs –
The stiff Heart questions was it He, that bore,
And Yesterday, or Centuries before?

The Feet, mechanical, go round –
A wooden way
Of Ground, or Air, or Ought –
Regardless grown,
A Quartz contentment, like a stone –

This is the Hour of Lead –
Remembered, if outlived,
As Freezing persons, recollect the Snow –
First – Chill – then Stupor – then the letting go …"

"After Great Pain" (1862) Emily Dickinson, American Poet, (1830-1886)

"Give sorrow words: the grief that does not speak
Whispers the o'er fraught heart, and bids it break."

"Macbeth" 1606-07 William Shakespeare, English Poet and Playwright (1564-1616)

"About suffering they were never wrong,
The Old Masters; how well they understood
Its human position; how it takes place
While someone else is eating or opening a window
Or just walking dully along."

W.H. Auden, English/ American Poet (1907-1973)
Copyright © 1940 by W.H. Auden renewed. Reprinted by permission of Curtis Brown Ltd.

"Things are unbearable,
just until we have them to bear."

George MacDonald, Scottish Author and Poet (1824-1905)

"For, if their life be lost, their toils are o'er,
And woe and want can trouble them no more ..."

"On Peaceful Death and Painful Life",
The Works of Patrick Branwell Bronte, Sonnet 111, Volume 3, 1837-1848
Patrick Branwell Bronte, English Writer and Painter (1817-1848)

"Let us not waste heart and life thinking of
what might have been and
forgetting the "may be" that lies before us."

"Idle Thoughts of an Idle Fellow" (1886) Jerome K. Jerome, English Writer (1859-1927)

"The foot less prompt to meet the morning dew,
The heart less bounding at emotion new,
And hope, once crushed, less quick to spring again."

"Thyrsis" (1865) Matthew Arnold, English Poet (1822-1888)

Daniel 1969 – 1981

"Come to me in my dreams, and then
By day I shall be well again –
For then the night will more than pay
The hopeless longing of the day."

"Faded Leaves – Longing" (1852) Matthew Arnold, English Poet (1822-1888)

"I shall walk in the Sun alone, whose golden light you loved.
I shall sleep alone and, stirring, touch an empty place.
I shall write uninterrupted.
(Would that your gentle paw could stir my moving pen just once again!)
I shall see beauty, but none to match your living grace.
I shall hear music but not so sweet as the droning song with which you loved me.
I shall fill my days but I shall not, cannot forget:
Sleep soft, dear friend, for while I live you shall not die."

"Charles The Story of a friendship – To a Siamese Cat " (1943)
Michael Joseph, British Publisher and Writer (1897-1958)

"I have done mostly what most men do,
And pushed it out of my mind;
But I can't forget, if I wanted to,
Four-Feet trotting behind.

Day after day the whole day through –
Wherever my road inclined –
Four-Feet said, "I am coming with you!"
And trotted along behind.

Now I must go by some other round –
Which I shall never find –
Somewhere that does not carry the sound
Of Four-Feet trotting behind."

"Four-Feet" from "Limits and Renewals" (1932) Rudyard Kipling,
English Poet and Novelist (1865-1936)

"I, who had had my heart full for hours, took
advantage of an early moment of solitude, to cry in it
very bitterly. Suddenly a little hairy head thrust
itself from behind my pillow into my face, rubbing its
ears and nose against me in a responsive agitation,
and drying the tears as they came."

Elizabeth Barrett Browning, English Poet (1806-1861)

"Never morning wore
To evening, but some heart did break."

"In Memoriam" (1850) Alfred, Lord Tennyson, English Poet (1809-1892)

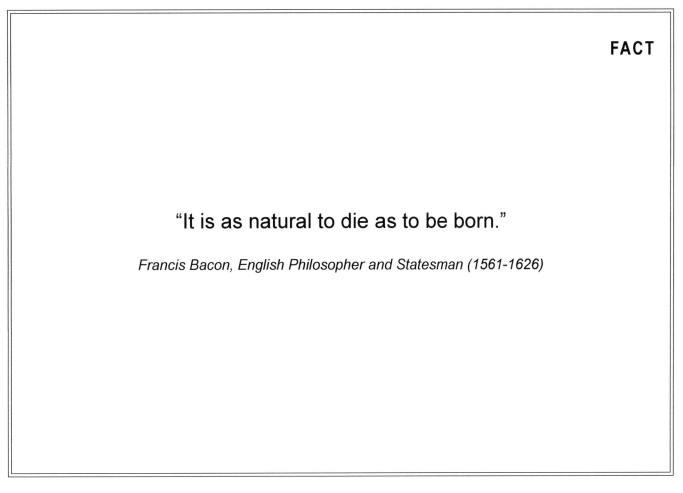

"It is as natural to die as to be born."

Francis Bacon, English Philosopher and Statesman (1561-1626)

"There should be no despair, though tears
May flow down like a river:
Are not the best beloved of years
Around your heart forever?"

"Sympathy" – Emily Bronte, English Novelist and Poet (1818-1848)

"The death of a dog is the end of an era."

Laura Chester, American Author and Poet (1949-)
First published in "Bitches Ride Alone" – Black Sparrow Press
Permission granted by Laura Chester

Cinders (1983-1998), Solo (1985-2000), Buttons (1983-1993)

"Not the least hard thing to bear when they go from us,
these quiet friends, is that they carry away with them
so many years of our own lives."

"Memories", 1929 John Galsworthy, English Novelist and Playwright (1867-1933)

"The two dogs were in very low spirits when they continued their journey without the cat. The old dog in particular moped badly, for the cat had been his constant close companion for many years – ever since the day when a small, furiously hissing kitten, with comically long black-stockinged legs and a nearly white body had joined the Hunter family. This apparition had refused to give one inch of ground to the furious and jealous bull terrier who was an avowed cat hater, and the terror of the nearby feline population; instead it had advanced, with every intention of giving battle evident in the tiny body. The dog, for the first and last time in his life, capitulated. That day a bond had been formed between them, and thereafter they had been inseparable."

"The Incredible Journey", 1961 Sheila Burnford, British Canadian Writer (1918-1984)
Permission granted by David Higham Associates Ltd.

".... and the ashes not soft as in imagination,
But like pellets almost.
We dump them among the rabbit droppings, and
Run through the mud and drizzle,
Back to nothing where something was before,
Leaving our royal one soaking into the soft downland grass
Faceless to the sky"

"Disposing of Ashes" – Elizabeth Bartlett, British Poet (1924-2008)
Permission granted from Bloodaxe Books

BURIAL

"There are various places within which a dog may be buried. We are thinking now of a setter, whose coat was flame in the sunshine, and who, so far as we are aware, never entertained a mean or an unworthy thought. This setter is buried beneath a cherry tree, under four feet of garden loam, and at its proper season the cherry strews petals on the green lawn of his grave. Beneath a cherry tree, or an apple, or any flowering shrub of the garden, is an excellent place to bury a good dog. Beneath such trees, such shrubs, he slept in the drowsy summer, or gnawed at a flavorous bone, or lifted head to challenge some strange intruder. These are good places, in life or in death. Yet it is a small matter, and it touches sentiment more than anything else.

For if the dog be well remembered, if sometimes he leaps through your dreams actual as in life, eyes kindling, questing, asking, laughing, begging, it matters not at all where that dog sleeps at long and at last. On a hill where the wind is unrebuked and the trees are roaring, or beside a stream he knew in puppyhood, or somewhere in the flatness of a pasture land, where most exhilarating cattle graze. It is all one to the dog, and all one to you, and nothing is gained, and nothing lost – if memory lives. But there is one best place to bury a dog. One place that is best of all.

If you bury him in this spot, the secret of which you must already have, he will come to you when you call – come to you over the grim, dim frontiers of death, and down the well-remembered path, and to your side again. And though you call a dozen living dogs to heel they should not growl at him, nor resent his coming, for he is yours and he belongs there. People may scoff at you, who see no lightest blade of grass bent by his footfall, who hear no whimper pitched too fine for mere audition, people who may never really have had a dog. Smile at them then, for you shall know something that is hidden from them, and which is well worth the knowing. The one best place to bury a good dog is in the heart of his master."

"Where to bury a dog" from "How could I be Forgetting" Permission granted by Binford & Mort Publishing

Ben Hur Lampman, American Newspaper Editor, Poet (1886-1954)

"Rosie, our beloved border collie –
Herder of children,
Protector of garden gate,
Walker of pensive writers and
Centre of family life –
Has died, aged 12.
R.I.P. best of dogs".

Robert Harris, English Novelist (1957 –)
Permission granted by "The Sunday Times" 3.6.2018

"Near this spot
Are deposited the remains of one
Who possessed beauty without vanity,
Strength without insolence,
Courage without ferocity,
And all the virtues of man without his vices.
This praise, which would be unmeaning flattery
If inscribed over human ashes,
is but a just tribute to the memory of
Boatswain, a Dog.
Who was born at Newfoundland, May, 1803
And died at Newstead, Nov. 18, 1808"

George Gordon, Lord Byron, English Poet (1788-1824)
Epitaph to his dog on a monument in the garden at Newstead Abbey

"No heaven will not ever
Heaven be
Unless my cats are there
To welcome me"

Anonymous Epitaph in a pet cemetery

"A Hero's goodbye for Marines service dog
Hundreds of people gathered at Michigan War Dog Memorial over the weekend for the
burial of Cena, a service dog that served three tours of Afghanistan with the
U.S. Marines… accompanied by three volleys of rifle fire".

Permission granted by the "i" newspaper, reported July 2017

Domino (1986-2006) and Buttons (1983-1993)

"To call him a dog hardly seems to do him justice,
though inasmuch as he had four legs, a tail and barked,
I admit he was, to all outward appearances.
But to those of us who knew him well,
he was a perfect gentleman."

Hermione Gingold, English Actress (1897-1987)
Extract from "My Own Unaided Work" (1952) describing her friend,
Hermione Baddeley's dog, Mr. Bags

"I hope the angels are feeding him
lots of fresh fish and that he is
snoozing in a celestial armchair."

Ann Widdecombe, former M.E.P. (1947 –)
Thoughts expressed on the death of her cat, Carruthers
Permission granted by Ann Widdecombe

"So I laugh when I hear them make it plain
That dogs and men never meet again.
For all their talk who'd listen to them
With the Soul in the shining eyes of him
Would God be wasting a dog like Tim?"

Winifred Mary Letts, English born writer (1882-1972)
permission granted by Oriana Conner, grandniece

"He was awake a long time
before he remembered that his heart was broken."

Ernest Hemingway, American Novelist (1899-1961)
From "The Short Stories of Ernest Hemingway" by Ernest Hemingway.
Copyright © 1927 by Charles Scribner's Sons. Copyright renewed © 1955 by Ernest Hemingway.
Reprinted with the permission of Scribner, a division of Simon & Schuster, Inc. All rights reserved.

"You have to believe in happiness
Or happiness never comes ….
Ah, that's the reason a bird can sing –
On his darkest day, he believes in Spring."

Douglas Malloch, American Poet (1877-1938)

"Oh what unhappy twist of fate
Has brought you homeless to my gate.
The gate where once another stood
To beg for shelter warmth and food.

For from that day I ceased to be
The master of my destiny.
While, he, with purr and velvet paw
Became within my house the law.

He scratched the furniture and shed
And claimed the middle of my bed.
He ruled in arrogance and pride
And broke my heart the day he died.

So, if you really think, oh cat
I'd willingly re-live all that,
Because you come forlorn and thin
Well don't just stand there – come on in!"

"Stray Cat" – Francis Witham   Permission granted by All-Creatures.org

"Which one would you like ….
How was I to know?
They all looked so enchantingly alike. As I hesitated one of the kittens detached itself
from the rest and with brave curiosity ran across the room towards me. I held out my hand,
gently, as one should do when greeting an animal. The kitten boldly approached,
looking up at me enquiringly. I stroked his soft coat and his tiny body quivered
responsively. He began to purr and rub against my hand.
I hesitated no longer. "This, I said, is my little cat".

"Charles – The Story of a friendship" (1943)
Michael Joseph, British Publisher and Writer (1897-1958)

"…..people who keep dogs (or cats, for that matter)
live longer on average than those who do not. This
Is not some kind of pro-canine campaigning fantasy.
It is a simple medical fact that the calming influence
of the company of a friendly pet animal reduces
blood pressure and therefore the risk of heart attack."

Desmond Morris, F.L.S., – English Zoologist, Ethologist, Surrealist Painter & Author (1928 –)
Permission granted by Desmond Morris

Domino(1986-2006) and Solo (1985-2000)

"No matter how tired or wretched I am,
A pussy-cat sitting in a doorway can divert my mind."

Mary E. Wilkins Freeman, American Author (1852-1930)

"It is by muteness that a dog becomes for one so
utterly beyond value; with him one is at peace,
where words play no torturing tricks . . .
Those are the moments that I think are precious to a
dog – when, with his adoring soul coming through
his eyes, he feels that you are really thinking of him."

John Galsworthy, English Novelist and Playwright (1867-1933)

"They are much superior to human beings as companions.
They do not quarrel or argue with you.
They never talk about themselves, but listen to you while you talk about yourself, and
keep up an appearance of being interested in the conversation.
They never make stupid remarks.
…They never say unkind things…
We are always the same to them."

"The Idle Thoughts of an Idle Fellow" (1886)
Jerome K. Jerome, English Writer (1859-1927)

"…Edward VII was almost inseparable from Caesar, his fox terrier…
At the King's funeral in May, 1910, it was recorded:
Immediately behind the gun carriage, which bore the coffin,
walked Caesar, followed by the German Emperor and eight kings".

Article in "The Sunday Times" 18.11.01
Permission granted by "The Sunday Times"

"Rich though he be in this world's goods
Poor is he in the end
Who in this life has never made
A faithful dog his friend."

Quoted in: "The love of a dog" (circa 1941)
Joan Gratiana Darell, English Author (1900-1985)

"Animals are such agreeable friends –
They ask no questions, they pass no criticisms."

"Scenes of Clerical Life Mr. Gilfil's Love Story" (1858)
George Eliot, English Novelist and Poet (1819-1880)

Billy 2000-2013

"To live in hearts we leave behind, is not to die"

"Hallowed Ground" (1797)
Thomas Campbell, Scottish Poet (1777-1844)